T st
Business English
Intermediate

Steve Flinders

Series Editor: Nick Brieger

D1147892

PENGUIN BOOKS

For Jerry Garcia (1

PENGUIN B

Published by the Penguin Group
Penguin Books Ltd, 27 Wrights Lane, London W8 5TZ, England
Penguin Putnam Inc., 375 Hudson Street, New York, New York 10014, USA
Penguin Books Australia Ltd, Ringwood, Victoria, Australia
Penguin Books Canada Ltd, 10 Alcorn Avenue, Toronto, Ontario, Canada M4V 3B2
Penguin Books (NZ) Ltd, 182–190 Wairau Road, Auckland 10, New Zealand

Penguin Books Ltd, Registered Offices: Harmondsworth, Middlesex, England

Published by Penguin Books 1997
10 9 8 7 6 5 4 3

Text copyright © Steve Flinders 1997
Illustrations copyright © Neville Swaine 1997
All rights reserved

Printed in England by Clays Ltd, St Ives plc
Set in 9.25/13.5pt Monophoto Times

Acknowledgements
Thanks to John Fagan, Susan Hunter, David Knowles, Chris Tanner and, in particular, Bob Dignen, for allowing me access to their training course notes once again; to Alan Tucker for advice on Oil and Gas, and Derek Utley on Telecoms; and to Jean-Michel Delory for his useful suggestions.

INTRODUCTION

Language knowledge and communication skills are the basic tools for developing competence in a foreign language. Vocabulary, together with a command of grammar and pronunciation, are the main components of language knowledge.

This series aims to develop the vocabulary required by professionals and pre-service students. The materials provide clear and simple test materials of around 500 key concepts and terms in various professional areas. Each book is devoted to one professional area, divided into eight sections. Each section, focusing on one topic area, tests the knowledge of both concepts and terms. The materials can be used as part of a language course for specialists or as a handy reference for self-study.

For the first books, we have chosen areas which are of significant current interest in the business world. Each has been written by an author with considerable practical experience in the field, and we hope that the series will prove a valuable aid to users.

ABOUT THIS BOOK

Test Your Business English: Intermediate is for two groups of learners: learners of Business English at intermediate level; and learners of general English who want to develop their knowledge of Business English. In both cases, it aims to help them:
• check their knowledge of core concepts and key terms (words and expressions) used in business
• see how these terms are used so that they can use them effectively and successfully themselves.

The book will also be a useful source of information for trainers who need to run courses in Business English at intermediate level.

The material has been designed for self-study or classroom use.

Organization of the material
The book is divided into eight sections and each section deals with a different area of Business English. In this way it is organized more like a textbook than a test book, with individual sections devoted to individual areas. We have chosen this organization so that, if they wish, learners can work through each section and see how terms group together. We believe this will help learners develop their range of expression in a structured and systematic way.

After the tests, there is a complete answer key followed by a full A–Z word list.

Using the material
The Contents page shows the eight main areas covered. Learners can either work through the book from the beginning or select sections according to their interests or needs. After each test, learners should check their answers. While working on a test, learners may come across unknown or unfamiliar words. This is an opportunity for them to check their understanding and extend their knowledge. So, a good dictionary of English as well as a more specialist dictionary will be useful companions to this volume. In this way the material in this book can be used both for testing and for teaching.

Selection of the terms

This book follows on from *Test Your Business English: Elementary*, which covers basic terms. The vocabulary chosen for this intermediate level book is, therefore, more complex and aims to extend the learner's knowledge to a higher level. All the terms chosen are directly relevant to the work of people working in a wide range of business contexts. Finally, the language model is predominantly British English.

Other titles in the series

Test Your Business English: Elementary

Test Your Business English: Hotel and Catering

Test Your Business English: Marketing

Test Your Business English: Finance

Test Your Business English: Accounting

Test Your Business English: Secretarial

(Each of these books tests core vocabulary in their respective areas.)

CONTENTS

1 Jobs

Match the business cards (1–12) with the job descriptions (a–l).

1 | **John Bagnall**
   Ministry of Transport

a) We have two teams calling possible clients to fix meetings with the reps.

2 | **Sarah Whitaker**
   General Practitioner

b) We try to adapt our courses to the needs of each individual learner.

3 | Sidney Mole
   BANK MANAGER

c) We deal with most users' problems by phone.

4 | Mary Somerville
   Management Consultant

d) I have the biology chair.

5 | Charley Simpson
   Civil Engineer

e) We do mainly children's titles and dictionaries.

6 | Rosemary Mell
   PUBLISHER

f) We examine and (usually) approve company accounts.

7 | **Jack Castle**
   Sales Representative

g) I'm a civil servant, working on government road policies.

8 | **Sally Blunkett**
   Telesales Manager

h) I specialise in advising on management reporting systems.

9 | Alan Murphy
   Technical Support

i) We are always ready to discuss lending possibilities with our clients.

10 | **Susan Reed**
    Trainer

j) I visit all my clients three or four times a year to tell them about our latest products.

11 | CAROLINE BEVAN
    Auditor

k) I build bridges.

12 | *Professor Alan Stevens*

l) I have about 1,500 patients on my list.

2 Responsibilities

Sidney Rimbaud is talking about his job responsibilities but is having problems with his prepositions. Complete the following sentences, where necessary, with a preposition from the box. Some of the sentences do not need an extra word.

after	in	on	out	to (x2)	with (x2)

1 I head .... the marketing department at Kazoulis Communications.

2 I report directly .... Mr Kazoulis himself.

3 I look .... a department of about 30 people.

4 I deal .... all the major aspects of the company's marketing strategy.

5 I liaise .... the other members of the management committee.

6 I listen carefully .... what our customers say.

7 I handle .... one or two of the major accounts myself.

8 I'm working .... a very important account at the moment.

9 I also monitor .... the general situation in the market place.

10 We carry .... market surveys regularly.

11 We test .... new products on groups of consumers.

12 I am also involved .... one or two of Mr Kazoulis's takeover projects.

3 Money

Read the text and then do the crossword.

If you think that keeping your money under the bed is not a good idea, then you probably have a bank account. In Britain, you can pay in money and you can withdraw money from a current account quite easily, and you can earn interest on a savings or deposit account. You can transfer money to other accounts and you can tell the bank to pay your electricity, telephone and other bills by standing order or direct debit.

   Every month, the bank will send you a statement which tells you your balance and by how much you are in the black or in the red. If you are overdrawn, you will probably have to pay interest on the debt.

   Banks are happy to provide other services to their customers. For example, when you want to go abroad, the bank will sell you travellers' cheques or quote you an exchange rate for buying and selling foreign currency. And it will issue you with a credit card to make paying for goods and services easier, provided the bank thinks you are a good credit risk.

Across
1 Plastic money.
5 The cost of buying foreign money.
6 A colourful way of talking about a positive amount in your account.
7 A colourful way of talking about a negative amount in your account.
8 You can earn this on a savings account.
10 Take money from an account.
11 This tells you how much you have in your account.
13 Put money into your account.

Down
2 Useful when abroad.
3 When money is taken automatically from your account.
4 When your account is in debit.
9 The amount you have in your account.
12 Move money from one account to another.

Section 1: Background to business

4 Pay

Match the form of revenue (1–11) with the right recipient (a–k).

1 grant	a) author
2 salary	b) senior manager
3 wage	c) laid off employee
4 commission	d) government
5 fees	e) blue-collar worker
6 dividend	f) retired employee
7 royalty	g) sales representative
8 stock option	h) student
9 pension	i) consultant
10 tax	j) shareholder
11 redundancy pay	k) white-collar worker

5 Educational background

Marcia Garcia tells us about her educational background. Complete each sentence with one of the words or phrases from the box below. You will need to put the verbs into the right tense.

apply	graduate (verb)	grant	higher degree
honours degree	job	option	PhD
place	primary school	scholarship	secondary school
stay on	study	subject	thesis

1 I started at .... in London when I was 5.

2 At the age of 11, I went on to .... , also in London.

3 At 17, I .... to university.

4 I got a .... at Manchester to .... Engineering.

5 In fact I was awarded a ....

6 But at the end of the first year I changed to another ....

7 I .... from university in 1988.

8 I have a first class .... in Economics.

9 I decided to .... at university.

10 So I did a .... in business administration at the University of California.

11 During the course, I did an .... on small business development.

12 I found the topic so interesting that I applied for a .... to do a doctorate on the same subject.

13 Once I had got the money, I had to write a 50,000 word ....

14 So now I have a BA, an MBA and a ....

15 All I need now is a ....

6 Geography

Kazoulis Communications is an international operation. Choose the correct expressions to describe its different locations.

We have operations in:

1 Birmingham in   a) the English Midlands   b) Middle England

2 Vienna in   a) Central Europe   b) the Centre of Europe

3 Dresden in   a) East Germany   b) the eastern part of Germany

4 Naples in   a) Southern Italy   b) South of Italy

5 Hong Kong in   a) the Far East   b) Far East

6 Bangkok in   a) South East Asia   b) the South Eastern Asia

7 New Delhi in   a) the Indian continent   b) the Indian sub-continent

8 San Francisco on   a) the West Coast   b) the Western Coast

9 California on   a) the Pacific Edge   b) the Pacific Rim

10 Boston on   a) the Eastern Seaboard   b) the Eastern Coast

11 Iowa City in   a) the Mid-East   b) the Mid-West

12 Riyadh in   a) the Mid-East   b) the Middle East

13 Lagos in   a) Western Africa   b) West Africa

We do business:

14 a) throughout the world   b) through all the world

15 a) across all the world   b) all over the world

7 Business initials

Write the full words for these sets of initials. The clues will help you.

1 OHP (for visual aids) ....

2 VCR (for home entertainment) ....

3 HQ (the centre of operations) ....

4 ROI (what you get back from the
money you put into a business) ....

5 PC (on your desk) ....

6 CEO (top job in the company) ....

7 JFK (an airport or a president) ....

8 GNP (a measure of national wealth) ....

9 DTP (software to produce your
own newsletter) ....

10 MBA (a qualification) ....

11 AGM (a meeting for shareholders) ....

12 VAT (a tax) ....

13 USP (what every company
should have) ....

14 AOB (the last item on the agenda) ....

8 Verbs

For each of the verbs below, three of the four words or expressions fit. In each case, circle the one which does not.

1 DO
   a) business
   c) your homework
   b) a profit
   d) a deal

2 MAKE
   a) money
   c) a loss
   b) business
   d) a decision

3 TAKE
   a) a long time
   c) appropriate measures
   b) a decision
   d) a deadline

4 HAVE
   a) progress
   c) shares in a company
   b) something to eat
   d) a meeting

5 MEET
   a) a deadline
   c) an appointment
   b) customers' expectations
   d) a target

6 LAUNCH
   a) a product
   c) a campaign
   b) a ship
   d) progress

7 COMPLETE
   a) a form
   c) a cheque
   b) a task
   d) a project

8 CARRY OUT
   a) an agreement
   c) research
   b) a plan
   d) a market survey

9 ACHIEVE
   a) progress
   c) a target
   b) a breakthrough
   d) little

10 REACH
   a) a decision
   c) an agreement
   b) a strategy
   d) a target

9 Verbs and nouns

Fit one verb from the box into each of the headlines (1–13) about Kazoulis in the business press.

bends	cuts	generates	implements
increases	launches	makes	meets
plays	reaches	runs	signs
sends			

1 **Expansion in US .... new business for Kazoulis.**

2 CHAIRMAN'S SPEECH .... CLEAR SIGNAL TO COMPETITORS.

3 *Kazoulis .... costs by closing regional offices.*

4 'KAZOULIS .... CLIENTS' NEEDS MORE EFFECTIVELY THAN EVER,' CHAIRMAN TELLS SHAREHOLDERS.

5 Kazoulis .... rules on advertising: questions in Parliament.

6 *Kazoulis .... big risk with latest share issue.*

7 *KAZOULIS .... SMALL PROFIT IN FOURTH QUARTER.*

8 KAZOULIS BOARD .... DECISION TO CLOSE REGIONAL OFFICES: BIG JOB LOSSES.

9 MANAGEMENT .... AGREEMENT WITH UNIONS ON NEW PAY AND CONDITIONS FOR KAZOULIS WORKFORCE.

10 Kazoulis .... leading role in advertising standards campaign.

11 **Kazoulis .... new product in youth market.**

12 **Chairman .... major contract with the Chinese.**

13 KAZOULIS .... MARKET SHARE AFTER CHINESE DEAL.

10 Adverbs

Fit one adverb from the box into each of the extracts from business documents or conversations (1–11).

absolutely	actively	conveniently	deeply
extensively	financially	highly	satisfactorily
tactfully	totally	unfairly	

1

> The new offices are ....
> situated close to the motorway and
> to the local railway station.

2

> I think what he said was
> unnecessary, inaccurate and
> .... unjustified.

3

> The new model has been
> .... tested and you will
> be impressed by its quiet operation,
> ease of use and elegant appearance.

4

> She said she had been
> .... dismissed but the
> court said her employer had been right
> to sack her.

5

> Now that the special project has been .... completed, we can all get on with our old jobs again.

6

> Dear Sir / Madam, I am .... seeking employment and wonder whether you have any vacancies in your accounts department at the moment.

7

> I think we should drop this project right now because I just don't believe that it's .... viable.

8

> Your performance in this office over the last two or three months has been .... unsatisfactory.

9

> I think the best thing you can do in the circumstances is to .... decline the offer.

10

> This book is .... recommended for anyone interested in the workings of international financial markets.

11

> Are you sure?

> I'm ....
> certain.

12

11 Prepositions

Supply the missing preposition(s) in each sentence.

at (x2)	between	by	in (x3)	into
on (x4)	to	over	under	

1
> Could you call back later? She's
> .... the other phone.

2
> It's not surprising that he's
> working less hard. He's very close
> .... retirement.

3
> They thought everything was
> .... control until they had a big
> dispute .... pay.

4
> There's clearly a strong link
> .... pay and productivity.

5
> The people on the shopfloor
> want more participation .... the
> decision-making process.

6

> We need a much stronger focus
> .... the needs of our
> customers.

7

> These meetings always start late.
> Could everyone make an effort to arrive
> .... time next time?

8

> I've divided this talk ....
> three main parts.

9

> It's impossible to say ....
> this stage .... the
> negotiation whether or not we will reach
> an agreement.

10

> We have to have all the figures
> .... the end of the month ....
> the very latest.

11

> We plan to achieve a 20%
> reduction .... the workforce before
> the end of the decade.

12

> I'm afraid she's not here – she's
> .... holiday until next Monday.

12 Two-part verbs

Look at the verbs below and decide which one goes with the words from list A or B. (See example):

	A	**B**
DRAW / DRAW UP	a conclusion	an agenda

You *draw* a conclusion
You *draw up* an agenda.

	A	**B**
1 OPEN / OPEN UP	a market	a letter
2 STAND / STAND FOR	drinks	an elected post
3 FALL / FALL DOWN	share prices	trees in storms
4 FILL / FILL IN	a form	with a sense of pride
5 CUT / CUT DOWN ON	cigarettes	costs
6 LAY / LAY OFF	workers	foundations
7 BREAK / BREAK UP	bad news	inefficient companies
8 SELL / SELL OFF	parts of a company	goods at a discount
9 KICK / KICK OFF	yourself	a meeting
10 TAKE / TAKE ON	extra staff	too long
11 PICK / PICK UP	the best person	a market can
12 BRING / BRING UP	a problem at a meeting	dynamism to the job
13 CARRY / CARRY OUT	duties	an important message

13 Adjectives and nouns

Some adjectives typically go with certain nouns. Fit the adjectives in the box below into the letter.

accurate	competitive	critical	easy	future
guaranteed	high	large	mixed	positive
right	valued	verbal		

Dear Marcelle

I am writing to you to thank you for another year of fruitful co-operation between our two companies. You are one of our most (1) .... customers and we always try to give you as (2) .... a level of service as possible at an extremely (3) .... price. We are sure that this is the (4) .... approach.

This is why we want you to be one of the first to know about our plans to improve our (5) .... prospects through expansion. We have already invested a (6) .... sum of money in up-to-date distribution facilities and negotiations for further financing are now entering a (7) .... stage. The result of all this will be (8) .... ordering, more (9) .... figures on the status of your orders, and (10) .... satisfaction for all.

Of course, there has been a (11) .... reaction from some of our newer customers, but I am sure that you will be patient with us during the period of transition.

These changes will make a (12) .... contribution to our continuing partnership and I can assure you that we shall continue to operate by (13) .... agreement on telephoned orders in the future as we have in the past.

Please contact me if you need more information.

With best regards

Alfredo

Alfredo McKay

Customer Relations Manager

14 Word building

Fill in the missing words in the table.

Verb	Person noun	General noun	Adjective
		administration	
			distributive
advise			
	constructor		
pay			
			soluble
		inspection	–
	promoter		
co-ordinate			–
		supervision	
		finance	

17

15 Spelling

Circle the correct spelling for each of the following words. In some cases, both versions are correct: which ones are they and why?

1	personnel	*or*	personell
2	address	*or*	adress
3	apraisal	*or*	appraisal
4	acommodation	*or*	accommodation
5	separate	*or*	seperate
6	reccomend	*or*	recommend
7	organise	*or*	organize
8	stationery	*or*	stationary
9	principle	*or*	principal
10	systematic	*or*	systemmatic
11	negociation	*or*	negotiation
12	comercial	*or*	commercial
13	hierarchy	*or*	heirarchy
14	enterprise	*or*	entreprise

16 Production

Plentiparts Inc. has been having production problems. Unscramble the words in capitals to make sense of the Production Manager's report.

1 At the beginning of the month we were O_ _ _ _ _ _ _G quite normally. (PRITENOAG)

2 There was plenty of S _ _ _ E C _ _ _ _ _ _ Y. (PREAS TPIYCAAC)

3 We had just I _ _ _ _ _ _ _ D some sophisticated new equipment. (LATSLENDI)

4 These were R _ _ _ _ S for the main A _ _ _ _ _ _ Y L _ _ E. (SBOORT / SYBLMASE NEIL)

5 Unfortunately, a problem developed with one of our main S _ _ _ _ _ _ _ S. (PURLIPESS)

6 They were our only source for a vital C _ _ _ _ _ _ _ T. (EMCPOTNON)

7 Normally they worked very well within our J _ _ _ – _ _ – _ _ _ E system (STUJ-NI-EMTI) and they could usually send an O _ _ _ R (RERDO) within 24 hours of our telephoning for a new C _ _ _ _ _ _ _ _ _ T. (GECNINMOSTN)

8 On this particular day, the D _ _ _ _ _ _ Y was late. (VILERYDE)

9 At the same time, there was a problem on one of the C _ _ _ _ _ _ R B _ _ _ S. (ROYVENOC STELB)

10 The S _ _ _ _ Y M _ _ _ _ _ R was out to lunch. (FEASTY ARMGENA)

11 The Q _ _ _ _ _ Y M _ _ _ _ _ R was away for the day. (LYTAUQI GRANAME)

12 No one reprogrammed the robots, and we ended up with a lot of F _ _ _ _ Y G _ _ _ S. (LUYTAF SODGO)

17 Marketing

Match the marketing terms (1–16) below with their definitions (a–p):

1 marketing	a) Change the image of a product or service.
2 niche	b) Aiming at the mass end of the market.
3 junk mail	c) A range of minor products which all carry the name of a major product.
4 hype	d) Aiming at the luxury end of the market.
5 brand	e) A promotional activity over a specific period of time.
6 upmarket	f) When a famous person recommends a product in an advertisement.
7 downmarket	g) Matching what the business organization produces with what customers want.
8 sponsorship	h) Promoting a product or service with exaggerated or intensive publicity.
9 crowded market	i) A small, specialised part of a market.
10 campaign	j) A product which can be recognized by its name.
11 reposition	k) When the same letter is sent to a large number of possible buyers.
12 pitch	l) Letters about products and services which you haven't asked for and probably don't want.
13 mailshot	m) One with too many competing products.
14 merchandising	n) A booklet giving information about the company's products or services.
15 endorsement	o) What the sales rep says to the potential customer.
16 brochure	p) Supporting a cultural or sporting enterprise in return for advertising.

18 Human Resources

Generosity Inc. has decided to improve the working conditions of its employees. Choose the correct term for each aspect of its new policy.

1 We will increase the amount of .... for women who are expecting babies.
   a) maternal leave   b) mothering leave c) maternity time   d) maternity leave

2 We will increase the size of the .... by 10%.
   a) manpower   b) workforce   c) human resources d) employees

3 We will give everyone .... training at least twice a year.
   a) in-house   b) tailoring   c) designed   d) outhouse

4 Night .... workers will get paid double time for working unsocial hours.
   a) owl   b) shift   c) time   d) group

5 There will be no more annual .... interviews.
   a) superior   b) appraisal   c) objective   d) holiday

6 We will pay everyone an extra .... at Christmas.
   a) salary   b) expense   c) commission   d) bonus

7 We will give .... employees the same status as full-timers.
   a) small time   b) part-time   c) short time   d) extra time

8 Employees will only have to give one week's .... before leaving.
   a) notice   b) delay   c) note   d) resignation

9 No one will be .... without the full agreement of the union.
   a) laid up   b) laid off   c) laid by   d) laid aside

10 Any future reductions in staff will be achieved only by ....
   a) natural   b) wasting away   c) natural wasting d) natural wastage
      tendencies

11 In future, promotion will be made purely on the basis of ....
   a) senior service   b) senior management c) seniority   d) senior status

12 Generous .... allowances will be paid when the company moves from the capital to a site in the provinces.
   a) restoration   b) restitution   c) relocation   d) refurbishment

19 Finance

Replace the words missing from the headlines in the financial press.

bankrupt	buyout	charges	currency	debt	dividend
flow	issue	losses	margins	profits	rates

1 **Shareholders rewarded with increased .... after good results at Megabuck.**

2 MOXWILL GOES .... : HUGE DEBTS UNCOVERED AFTER POLICE INVESTIGATION.

3 *........................... improve at Macrocomp after steep price rises.*

4 **JAYBURG FORCED TO WRITE OFF BAD .... AFTER MAIN SUPPLIER FAILS.**

5 **Pre-tax .... up at Flinco after improved trading in Far East.**

6 *SINGLE EUROPEAN .... WOULD BOOST TRADE, MINISTER CLAIMS.*

7 **'BANK .... TOO HIGH,' SAY NATIONAL BUSINESS LEADERS.**

8 HIGH INTEREST .... KILLING SMALL BUSINESS, SAYS MANAGEMENT GURU.

9 **Lonrev announce big share .... to finance planned expansion.**

10 **Bigbank finances management .... at Natbus.**

11 NEGATIVE CASH .... CREATES PROBLEMS FOR PERTH AND STEWART.

12 *Massive .... at Guam Investments after South American operation fails.*

20 Legal

Read the text and then do the crossword.

It is important for business people, especially small business people, to know something about the law, in particular, about their country's property legislation, since many companies have property contracts of different kinds. It is important to know what your company's legal liabilities are. Your company may own its own factories and office buildings and may lease some of its property to paying tenants. It may itself lease property from a landlord. In both cases, the small business person should know the details of each article of the contract to avoid breaches on either side. If either party does something illegal, then there is the danger that the other party will sue for breach of contract. The party with the weaker case might then do well to agree to an out-of-court settlement to stop the case from going on for too long. If you do not and the court's judgement goes against you, you may have to pay all the costs of the case.

   Another important area of commercial law is the law on patents, which protect the company's intellectual property. This area can be so complicated, however, that companies have to hire or train specialists to deal with it.

Across
1 An agreement which ends a dispute, sometimes made out of court.
4 The court's decision on a case.
5 An agreement for someone to use a property for a certain period of time in exchange for a regular payment.
7 You have this when you are legally responsible for something.
8 A formal legal agreement, usually in writing.
11 The opposite of legal.
12 This is when someone breaks a formal written agreement.

Down
2 The laws passed by a country's parliament.
3 To take legal action against someone in a civil case.
6 A part of a written legal agreement.
7 A man who rents land or property to someone.
9 Someone who pays rent on land or property.
10 This gives you the right to make and sell an invention.
13 The money paid by someone who loses a court case to cover the cost of the trial.

21 Research and Development

Supply the missing words from the box in these extracts from a British newspaper story about R& D. In two of the spaces, two answers are acceptable.

budget	centres	corporate	costs
evaluation	outsourcing	performance	policy
programmes	resources	spending	

R & D IN THE UK – THE CURRENT PICTURE

R & D (1) .... in the UK was £7.4bn. in 1995 and drugs companies accounted for 34% of all (2) .... British R & D. A study of R & D (3) .... methods has identified around 100 different approaches to the issue. One R & D (4) .... measure, adopted by Pilkington, the UK glass company, is to assess the current benefits of past research in terms of cost savings, licencing income and the profitability of new products.

The most important development in UK government R & D (5) .... has been the development of a new State-supported venture called Technology Foresight. This programme tries to identify the areas where the public and private sectors should concentrate their R & D (6) .... 'We want to translate the findings of TF into practical, useful R & D (7) .... ,' said a government minister.

Meanwhile in the electronics sector, escalating R & D (8) .... is one reason for the number of mergers in the industry. Amalgamation then often leads to the closure of some of the new company's R & D (9) .... ; a rationalisation of the company's R & D activities; and a reduction in the company's R & D (10) .... Other companies have started (11) .... R & D, sub-contracting at least some of their research work to contract research organisations (CROs).

22 Pricing

Read the following report and complete the text using words and expressions from
the box.

bulk	cost	down	grocery	margins
match	overcharging	overheads	policy	players
retail	undercutting	share	shakeout	war

In 1996, a price (1) .... broke out in one major Western economy
between the oil companies and supermarket retailers. A number of major oil
companies took the decision to switch to a low price (2) .... and to
(3) .... the prices of the retailers who up until then had been
significantly (4) .... the oil companies and who, as a result, had
succeeded in capturing a market (5) .... of about 25%. The retail
price in some parts of the country was already so low that the petrol companies said
that the supermarkets were selling petrol at below (6) .... It is,
however, unlikely that the supermarkets were doing this. More likely, they were able
to buy in (7) .... and to sell at low (8) .... since the
additional (9) .... involved in running a petrol station on an existing
supermarket site are small.

   The result of all this was an industry (10) .... which saw the
departure of a number of the smaller (11) .... in the petrol
(12) .... market. Supermarket chiefs responded by saying that the
petrol companies had been (13) .... customers for some time and that
they welcomed the challenge. 'We will respond in the same way as for any other
(14) .... price,' said a representative for one big chain. 'If we have to
come (15) .... in price, we will.'

SECTION 4: BUSINESS EXPRESSION

23 Word pairs

Use a word from the box to complete each of these business book titles.

bargaining	billing	conferences	drawbacks
exhibitions	fringe benefits	hunches	manuals
overheads	piloting	redundancy	regulations

1

> The NEW
> Business Guide
> to Trials and
> ....
> new products

2

> *Invoicing and*
> ....
> *for the modern business*

3

> The
> **1997**
> Guide to
> International
> Medical
> Congresses and
> ....

4

> *Increase your perks and*
> ....
> *NOW!*

5

The Writer's
Guide to
Writing **User
Guides** and
Technical

....

6

Managing

LARGE
SCALE

Layoffs and

....

7

*RUNNING COST
REDUCTION
AND CONTROL
OF*

....

**for non-financial
managers**

8

Successful
Negotiating
and

....

*for
Trade Unionists*

9

INTUITIONS

AND

....

WHICH CHANGED
THE DIRECTION OF

CORPORATE
AMERICA

10

101
Disadvantages and

....

**you Face
if you Ignore the
Benefits of Corporate
Re-Engineering**

11

*Health &
Safety
Rules
and*

....

12

How to

succeed

at International
Trade Fairs and

....

24 Word families

Circle the odd one out in each of these groups of business words and phrases. (See example):

1 a) check b) survey c) control d) monitor

2 a) sack b) dismiss c) demote d) fire

3 a) predict b) forecast c) anticipate d) analyse

4 a) lay off b) employ c) take on d) recruit

5 a) rewrite b) redraft c) reword d) restore

6 a) timetable b) plan c) strategy d) policy

7 a) banned b) prohibited c) postponed d) forbidden

8 a) cancel b) put off c) put back d) postpone

9 a) busy b) engaged c) tied up d) unavailable

10 a) You're welcome b) Not at all c) It was a pleasure d) Excuse me

11 a) nearly six b) about six c) sixish d) around six

25 Problem pairs

These pairs of words often cause problems. Choose the correct alternative for each.

1 SUBSIDY / SUBSIDIARY
 a) Kazoulis Communications is losing money and wants the government to give it a ....
 b) Our head office is in Boston and we own 70% of a manufacturing .... in Colorado.

2 POLICY / POLITICS
 a) Rimbaud has been sacked! People are saying he's a victim of internal ....
 b) If we want to convince the public that we care for the environment, we need to change our .... on dumping waste into the local river.

3 ECONOMIC / ECONOMICS
 a) She studied .... at university and is now an economist with a big international bank.
 b) She analyses the general .... problems faced by companies operating within traditional industries like shipbuilding.

4 ECONOMY / ECONOMIES
 a) Their government is trying to liberalize the .... while keeping tight political control.
 b) Overheads are getting out of control and we need to make major .... right across the business.

5 COMPLIMENTARY / COMPLEMENTARY
 a) We got some .... tickets for the big golf tournament through their corporate hospitality programme.
 b) We got some very .... remarks from the people who came to the golf tournament through our corporate hospitality programme.

6 NOTE / NOTICE
 a) He left a .... on my desk saying he would be late for the meeting.
 b) He put a .... on the board in the main corridor saying that the meeting had been postponed to 3 o'clock.

7 MORAL / MORALE

a) .... has been at rock bottom ever since they announced the job cuts.

b) When a company sacks such a huge number of people, it's not just an economic question; it becomes a .... question as well.

8 SAFETY / SECURITY

a) The .... officer has just been round the site with his dog checking all the locks and cameras.

b) The .... officer insists on all employees wearing the right kinds of protective clothing at all times.

9 TAKE OVER / OVERTAKE

a) They want to .... our company but I don't think their offer is high enough for our shareholders to sell.

b) They expect to .... all their main competitors, in terms of sales, within a year of the launch of their new product.

26 Opposites

Fit each term from the box – the opposite of the <u>underlined</u> word – into one of the extracts from business discussions (1–14).

cons	contract	decline	divest	fall
fire	lay off	loss	peripheral	reduce
weaknesses	withdraw			

1 'We have to debate the <u>pros</u> and .... of this project before we go ahead with it.'

2 'Let's look at the <u>strengths</u> and .... of each application in turn and then we'll draw up a shortlist.'

3 'We expect a <u>rise</u> in sales next year followed by a steady .... for two years after that.'

4 'It's simple: we have to <u>increase</u> our prices and .... our costs.'

5 'You can see the general position if you look at the <u>profit</u> and .... account in front of you.'

6 'Those were the golden years, ladies and gentlemen, when we saw the company <u>expand</u> rapidly and successfully. Unfortunately, demand turned down and we were then forced to .... our operations to something approaching our current size.'

7 'We had managed to <u>deposit</u> quite a large sum of money in our account at the beginning of the month but then we had to .... it almost immediately.'

8 'We need to concentrate on our <u>core</u> business and sell off our .... businesses.'

9 'It's easier to <u>hire</u> people when times are good than to .... them when times are hard.'

10 'We had hoped to <u>accept</u> your kind invitation to visit your plant next month but unfortunately we are obliged to .... your offer due to a change of plan.'

11 'Our strategy is to <u>acquire</u> large, inefficient companies and then .... them of their smaller profitable parts at a profit.'

12 'Although we have been able to <u>recruit</u> a handful of skilled workers for our main factory, we have also had to .... several hundred office staff.'

27 Idioms

Match the idioms (1–10) with their meanings (a–j).

1 They should never have tried to <u>sweep</u> that pollution scandal <u>under the carpet</u>.

    a) dangerous situation

2 That company will go bankrupt if they don't cut some red tape.

    b) all the time

3 At the end of our presentation, he spent ten minutes pouring cold water on our proposal.

    c) be treated unfairly

4 The head of research herself agreed to be the guinea pig for the trials on the new drug.

    d) no conditions

5 We agreed to do exercises every morning but we drew the line at wearing the company uniform.

    e) refused

6 We must be very careful about promoting ourselves as an ethical company – we're in a minefield!

    f) hide something

7 Chivers is going to damage his health – he's been working round the clock.

    g) adopt good tactics

8 It's yours for a million and no strings attached.

    h) bureaucracy

9 They could get the contract if they play their cards right.

    i) be discouraging

10 It looks as if Teddy got a raw deal.

    j) experimental subject

28 Business sectors

Match the companies on the left (1–16) with their sectors on the right (a–p).

1 A company which makes aspirin.	a) automotive
2 A company which mines diamonds.	b) construction
3 A company which makes men's suits.	c) consumer electronics
4 A company which sells package holidays.	d) catering
5 A company which makes trucks.	e) defence
6 A company which distributes electricity.	f) extractive
7 A supermarket chain.	g) fast food
8 A company which builds houses.	h) media
9 A company which makes washing machines.	i) pharmaceuticals
10 A company which sells hamburgers.	j) retail
11 A company which makes camcorders.	k) textiles
12 A road haulage company.	l) toiletries
13 A company which makes fighter planes.	m) tourism
14 A company which makes shampoo.	n) transport
15 A restaurant chain.	o) utilities
16 A newspaper publisher.	p) white goods

29 Telecommunications

Choose the correct option (*a*, *b*, *c* or *d*) to complete each sentence.

1 Privatisation of state telecommunications companies is just one part of the worldwide move towards telecoms ....
   a) deregulation   b) administration   c) networks   d) communication

2 .... technology is rapidly replacing analogue in mobile telephony.
   a) Communication b) Digital   c) Roaming   d) Global

3 Four strands of .... , each about the thickness of a human hair, can carry up to 600,000 telephone conversations at the same time.
   a) cordless phone   b) twisted wire   c) copper cable   d) optical fibre

4 Life is becoming more and more competitive for equipment ....
   as investment costs and the number of mergers increase.
   a) manufacturers   b) users   c) regulators   d) operators

5 Some countries with very old .... networks may decide not to invest in these but to go straight into the development of a sophisticated mobile system instead.
   a) optical   b) privatised   c) digital   d) fixed

6 .... satellites orbit the Earth, staying in the same place relative to the Earth's surface.
   a) Radio   b) Geostationary   c) Medium-earth orbiter   d) Low-earth orbiter

7 Users can now .... calls, that is, transfer them to another number.
   a) forward   b) reverse   c) charge   d) postpone

8 You can have your mobile system .... in order to stop other people listening in on your conversations.
   a) upgraded   b) encrypted   c) bugged   d) debugged

9 When your mobile phone is switched on, ready to receive calls, it is
   ....
   a) on standby   b) on duty   c) on full alert   d) on guard

10 At the heart of any telecoms system is the .... system where call-processing and subscriber-related functions are located.
   a) operation   b) support   c) switching   d) base station

30 Insurance

Read the text and then do the crossword.

If you are worried about the cost to you or your business of events such as accident, fire, theft or death, then you can take out an insurance policy. You can either go directly to an insurance company or you can talk to a broker, who will help you decide which company has the best policy for you. First you say what you want your insurance to cover, then the broker will tell you which policy he or she thinks you should take out. The broker will tell you how much money or premium you will have to pay for the cover you want, so that you can get money back from the insurer if an accident happens.

   If an accident does happen, you make a claim to your broker or to the insurance company directly. If the company agrees to your claim, you receive money. This is the settlement of your claim. In the case of a claim on an assured life, the beneficiary – the person who gets the money when someone dies – is usually a member of the policyholder's family.

   A pension plan is another kind of insurance. You pay a regular contribution, for example every month, and when you retire, the company pays you a pension. A company scheme which employees have to join is called a mandatory plan.

Across

 1 Start a policy with an insurance company. (4, 3)
 5 The regular sum of money you receive after you retire. (7)
 6 The agreement which you and the company sign. (6)
 9 Someone who gives advice about the best insurance available. (6)
10 The person who gets money from an insurance company, for example when
    someone dies. (11)
11 A compulsory plan, one that you have to be part of. (9)
12 The money you pay to the insurance company for cover. (7)
13 The demand you make to the insurance company when there is an accident. (5)
14 'Insured' for life. (7)

Down

2 An unexpected event which may result in injury or even death to person or injury to property. (8)

3 The regular sum of money paid into your pension plan. (12)

4 The protection you get from the insurance company. (5)

7 When the company agrees to your claim. (10)

8 The kind of insurance for which the insurance company pays money when someone dies. (4)

31 Banking and investment

Here are ten headlines and opening sentences from stories taken from the financial press. Fit one word or phrase from the box into each headline.

bank crisis	commodities	Derivatives
Developing World	Earnings	Forex
interest rates	mergers and acquisitions	portfolios
tariffs		

1 ANALYSTS FORECAST DIFFICULT YEAR FOR ....

Experts are predicting increasing volatility in the markets for some metals following news of an attempted coup d'état in Flingolia.

2 **Federal Reserve moves on** ....

All eyes are today on the leading European Central Banks to see how they respond to yesterday's cut in American rates.

3 *BIG FUNDS DIVERSIFYING* ....

Institutional investors are moving into Far Eastern and East European markets in an attempt to spread their risks over a wider range of equities than has been fashionable recently.

4 .... *trading down today*

The dollar gained significantly today, largely at the expense of the Deutschmark, during brisk trading which also saw heavy dealing in Swiss francs and sterling.

5 .... **strengthen**

Somewhat to the surprise of commentators, the London markets saw futures moving ahead during an afternoon of busy trading.

6 *MAJOR BANK TO REVIEW* .... *LOANS*

Sir David Marsh, chairman of National Central, announced that Natcen would be looking again at its lending policies, following the default of three leading financial institutions in Flingolia, one of the poorest states in the continent.

7 .... **at Kazoulis fall short of market projections**

Fourth quarter results have seriously disappointed observers, and the demonstrations by angry shareholders outside the company's head office symbolise the company's current problems.

8 MOVE TO AVERT ISADORIAN ....

The growing problem of bad debts, combined with uncertainties about the result of the forthcoming elections, is shaking public confidence in the nation's financial institutions.

9 *West Africans to cut* ....

In a historic agreement signed yesterday, the seven states involved in the talks, have agreed to move towards a free trade zone over a period of just three years.

10 **POOR YEAR FOR** ....

Not only has the market been very sluggish, but also competition for M & A business is hotting up and some of the smaller players are finding it more and more difficult to survive.

32 Entertainment and media

Find a word in the word square on the next page which means:

1 To send out a radio or TV programme.

2 A big media company possibly with TV as well as newspaper and magazine interests. (two words)

3 This category refers to popular newspapers. (two words)

4 This category refers to serious newspapers. (two words)

5 Advertising spots on TV.

6 A kind of TV programme where famous people talk to the host and each other, usually about themselves. (two words)

7 A kind of TV programme where people compete for prizes, often by answering quiz questions. (two words)

8 A kind of TV series about the lives of a group of people which often runs for a long time.

9 A company which makes films is often called this.

10 A company which brings films to the cinema.

11 The American word for film.

12 An underground system for bringing TV programmes into the home.

13 A TV system which uses a dish to receive the programmes.

14 Many TVs can receive up to 50 of these now.

The answers read vertically, horizontally and diagonally within the box.

X	V	L	D	I	S	T	R	I	B	U	T	O	R	K	D	S	P	J	B
S	S	M	E	F	H	O	O	L	G	O	J	M	N	I	O	B	O	C	B
T	T	F	D	I	N	E	T	U	V	K	I	H	S	N	C	A	P	A	M
G	C	U	T	O	N	G	A	J	W	Q	O	K	A	D	L	C	Q	W	P
B	H	A	D	E	A	P	B	U	F	U	P	X	T	M	O	R	V	S	I
I	R	S	R	I	T	I	L	P	E	A	F	Q	E	N	P	O	J	A	M
M	A	C	I	N	O	B	O	D	E	L	Z	L	L	R	I	Q	D	K	O
E	W	O	R	R	Q	U	I	A	D	I	G	K	L	Y	Q	Y	R	X	V
D	O	T	A	N	S	B	D	M	A	T	H	G	I	H	S	Z	X	L	I
I	P	F	O	J	E	H	P	O	C	Y	A	J	T	T	F	E	S	Y	E
A	U	R	G	I	K	R	R	Q	E	P	C	B	E	F	G	U	W	N	A
E	L	C	V	E	E	D	E	A	B	R	D	I	J	Z	A	V	M	V	H
M	I	H	A	N	T	Y	S	C	H	E	E	C	H	A	N	N	E	L	S
P	V	J	P	B	A	W	S	P	A	S	H	F	U	V	T	B	U	M	L
I	M	K	R	V	L	Y	N	O	X	S	I	C	H	A	T	S	H	O	W
R	E	N	O	W	L	E	W	W	A	G	Y	B	G	Z	S	C	T	W	J
E	R	S	L	U	M	S	M	F	C	O	M	M	E	R	C	I	A	L	S
T	E	N	S	L	T	E	N	O	N	E	X	U	P	H	Q	T	S	D	X
U	B	R	O	A	D	C	A	S	T	F	O	V	I	T	U	R	Z	I	G
Z	C	O	R	Y	D	R	P	J	Z	Y	G	A	M	E	S	H	O	W	K

33 Oil and gas

The words (1–19) show the right order of stages in oil production. <u>Match</u> (a–s) on the right with the correct numbers on the left to make a complete passage.

1 Carry out	a) the crude into intermediate products.
2 Obtain	b) the crude to bring it up to the refinery specification.
3 Drill	c) the oil bearing layers.
4 Analyse	d) them in large storage tanks. Then
5 Evaluate	e) a licence for exploratory drilling.
6 determine	f) the production platform and pipeline.
7 quantify	g) the petrol by truck to the service station and
8 Select	h) them into finished products and
9 Draw up	i) the underground reservoir in order to
10 Install	j) the petrol by pipeline to a regional storage depot,
11 Process	k) an initial development plan.
12 Pump	l) the data from the exploratory drilling.
13 Load	m) geological studies and seismic surveys.
14 distill	n) the size, shape and structure of the accumulation and to
15 Blend	o) to the motorist.
16 store	p) it into tankers and
17 convey	q) the most suitable recovery process.
18 deliver	r) an exploration well.
19 sell	s) the crude oil ashore.

34 Pharmaceuticals

Choose the correct option (*a, b, c, d*) to complete each sentence.

1 So many mergers are taking place within the pharmaceuticals industry that there
may soon be only five or six major .... operating
worldwide.
   a) conglomerations   b) agglomerates   c) conglomerates   d) agglomerations

2 All the major groups are currently looking for the .... remedies of
the twenty-first century which will keep their profits at current levels.
   a) blockbuster   b) roller coaster   c) bread and butter d) over-the-counter

3 This is why the number of alliances between the pharmaceutical companies and
.... groups is increasing.
   a) high technology   b) biotechnology   c) intermediate   d) medicare
                                                technology

4 Maintaining profits is becoming more difficult for pharmaceutical companies as
more and more governments introduce policies of ....
   a) health and safety b) welfare reform   c) health care   d) social security
                                                reform   reform

5 Ordinary .... are being encouraged to become more
cost conscious.
   a) general   b) specialists   c) medical orderlies d) company doctors
      practitioners

6 They are now expected as far as possible to write .... for cheaper,
rather than for more expensive drugs.
   a) inscriptions   b) conscription   c) recipes   d) prescriptions

7 The cost and the length of .... for possible new molecules is also
   increasing.
   a) government   b) clinical trials   c) medical   d) pilot projects
      tests   examinations

8 While the requirements of .... such as the US Food and Drug
   Administration are still very strict.
   a) registrars   b) regulars   c) regulators   d) rule makers

9 In addition, ... are expiring on a number of previous best sellers.
   a) copyrights   b) protection   c) patents   d) trademarks

10 For both these reasons, the market in .... drugs is one of the
   healthiest in the sector.
   a) general   b) generic   c) genetic   d) genial

11 The big companies are also taking the .... market more and more
   seriously.
   a) do-it-yourself   b) just-in-time   c) over-the-counter d) user-friendly

35 Conferences

Complete the letter to Dr Stimic by choosing the right word (a–d) for each of the gaps (1–10).

Dear Dr Stimic

We would like you to be the (1) .... speaker at our next international management (2) .... We would like you to give a forty minute (3) .... on the subject of (4) .... in International Management in the Nineties. This will be the subject of the (5) .... which will open this annual five-day event. The (6) .... will be composed largely of senior managers and management consultants. We should like to propose a (7) .... of $1,000 for your talk plus expenses.

If you are happy to accept, I should be grateful if you would let me know what (8) .... you will need for your talk. In addition, I am pleased to be able to offer your company, Stimic Consultants, a discounted rate for a (9) .... in the conference (10) ....

I hope you will be able to accept our invitation and I look forward to hearing from you soon.

Yours sincerely

J. A. Poborsky

Jerry A. Poborsky, Secretary General, Association of International Executives

1 a) keyhole   b) keynote   c) turnkey   d) keyboard

2 a) conference   b) exhibition   c) trade fair   d) party

3 a) seminar   b) workshop   c) session   d) paper

4 a) Tests   b) Tendencies   c) Trends   d) Subjects

5 a) plenary session b) whole session c) big talk   d) split session

6 a) crowd   b) spectators   c) onlookers   d) audience

7 a) commission   b) royalty   c) fee   d) pay

8 a) aids   b) equipment   c) material   d) helps

9 a) pavilion   b) shop   c) stand   d) floor

10 a) market   b) fair   c) forum   d) exhibition

36 Presentations 1

Suzy Capra wants to give a good presentation so she has made a list of some of the things she wants to say. Unfortunately she has dropped all her language cards (a–j) on the floor. Help her to put them in the right order by matching them with the cues (1–10).

Cues

1 Give SUBJECT of presentation.
2 QUESTIONS OK.
3 LEAD INTO Part 1: History.
4 SUMMARIZE and close Part 1.
5 LINK to Part 2: Options.
6 VISUAL AID: show figures (transparency).
7 Summarize and CLOSE Part 2.
8 MOVE ON to Part 3: Recommendations.
9 CLOSE.
10 INVITE further QUESTIONS.

Language cards

a)

Now I'd like to move on to the choices we face today.

b)

Let's now move on to the option which I personally ...

c)

Thank you for your attention.

d)

Does anyone have anything to ask or to comment on?

e)

Please interrupt if
you have anything
you'd like to ask.

f)

To sum up, the
past record of
this project is...

g)

So let's start with
some background
information to
explain...

h)

As you can see,
the results are...

i)

I want to talk
to you today
about...

j)

That's all I want
to say about the
current alternatives.

37 Presentations 2

Match the pictures (1–12) with the instructions for making good presentations (a–l).

a) It is important to maintain eye contact with the people you are talking to.
b) Clearly signal the structure of your talk during the introduction.
c) Select and order your material carefully during the preparation stage of your presentation.
d) Use the right body language to get your message across.
e) Dress appropriately.
f) Difficult questions should always be handled politely and diplomatically.
g) Establish a positive relationship with your audience as quickly as possible.
h) People will lose interest if you do not move your talk along at a lively pace.
i) Take a few deep breaths before you start, to help you overcome your initial nervousness.
j) Use your voice effectively to keep people involved.
k) Make sure your visual aids are clear and easy to follow.
l) Design and position your notes so that you can refer to them easily at all times.

38 Meetings

Put the quotes (a–s) in the right order according to the report of the meeting (1–19).

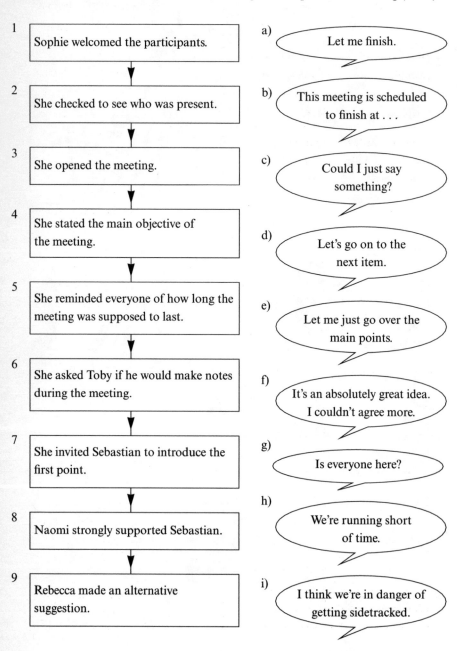

1 Sophie welcomed the participants.

2 She checked to see who was present.

3 She opened the meeting.

4 She stated the main objective of the meeting.

5 She reminded everyone of how long the meeting was supposed to last.

6 She asked Toby if he would make notes during the meeting.

7 She invited Sebastian to introduce the first point.

8 Naomi strongly supported Sebastian.

9 Rebecca made an alternative suggestion.

a) Let me finish.

b) This meeting is scheduled to finish at . . .

c) Could I just say something?

d) Let's go on to the next item.

e) Let me just go over the main points.

f) It's an absolutely great idea. I couldn't agree more.

g) Is everyone here?

h) We're running short of time.

i) I think we're in danger of getting sidetracked.

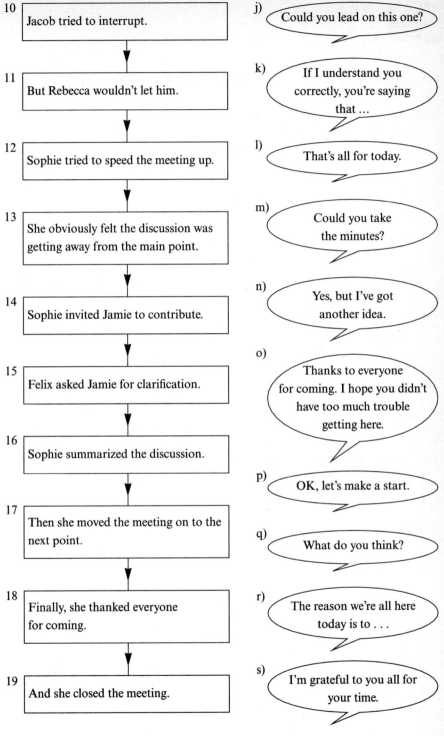

10 Jacob tried to interrupt.	**j)** Could you lead on this one?
11 But Rebecca wouldn't let him.	**k)** If I understand you correctly, you're saying that …
12 Sophie tried to speed the meeting up.	**l)** That's all for today.
13 She obviously felt the discussion was getting away from the main point.	**m)** Could you take the minutes?
14 Sophie invited Jamie to contribute.	**n)** Yes, but I've got another idea.
15 Felix asked Jamie for clarification.	**o)** Thanks to everyone for coming. I hope you didn't have too much trouble getting here.
16 Sophie summarized the discussion.	**p)** OK, let's make a start.
17 Then she moved the meeting on to the next point.	**q)** What do you think?
18 Finally, she thanked everyone for coming.	**r)** The reason we're all here today is to . . .
19 And she closed the meeting.	**s)** I'm grateful to you all for your time.

39 Telephoning

The staff of this company are having problems with their prepositions on the telephone: *some* of the prepositions in these sentences are wrong. Find the wrong ones and put the correct preposition in the space after the sentence. Choose from the following words. Some words are used more than once.

up	off	down	on	through	back

1 'Just a minute while I look up his number in the company phone book.'
  (LOOK ....)

2 'I'm sorry I can't talk to you now. Could I call you back in five minutes?'
  (CALL ....)

3 'I'm trying to get off to Mr Schmidt. Could you give me his extension number?'
  (GET ....)

4 'I need to take down his name and number.'
  (TAKE ....)

5 'Could you hang on a minute while I get a pen?'
  (HANG ....)

6 'I was talking to Mrs Bazin when we were cut up.'
  (CUT ....)

7 'Please could you put me down again?'
  (PUT ....)

8 'I've been trying to talk to her all day but every time I call she hangs back.'
  (HANGS ....)

9 'The phone rang and I picked off the receiver straightaway.'
  (PICKED ....)

10 'I'm sorry I don't have this information right now. Can I get up to you tomorrow?'
  (GET ....)

40 **Letters**

Match each of the following extracts from business letters (1–11) with the type of letter (a–k) from which it is taken.

1

> Mr Kazoulis would like a double room with shower and full board from 12 to 14 September inclusive.

2

> I am extremely sorry about the incident last week during the visit of your representative to our offices. Unfortunately . . .

3

> **THIS IS NOT THE FIRST TIME THAT THIS HAS HAPPENED AND I MUST INFORM YOU THAT IF IT HAPPENS AGAIN WE SHALL BE COMPELLED TO ISSUE A FORMAL REPRIMAND.**

4

> *I regret to inform you that your application for the post of Deputy Catering Manager has been unsuccessful. Thank you for . . .*

5

> Please find enclosed my CV and a recent photograph.

6

> I should be grateful if you would send me more information about your LK range of products including details of prices and discounts.

55

7

Thank you for your letter of 9 June. Please find enclosed a price list and full details of . . .

8

Please would you send to the above address 37 units of product reference number 37/LK/45006 (brown) and dispatch the invoice to our West Central office in the usual way.

9

Kazoulis Communications would be pleased to welcome Udo Schmidt to the opening of its new . . .

10

With reference to oustanding invoice number 9602132/64, we should be grateful if you would settle . . .

11

I wish to draw your attention to the very poor treatment our representative received when she called on you last week.

a) letter of invitation

b) response to an enquiry

c) letter requesting payment

d) letter of rejection

e) letter of apology

f) letter of enquiry

g) letter of application

h) letter of complaint

i) letter of warning

j) order

k) reservation

41 Forms

Name each form by writing in the missing word. One of the missing words appears twice.

1 'She already has two children and ten years' service so she'll get quite a lot of time off this time.'
(.............................. LEAVE FORM)

2 'I'd like to take a week at Easter and two weeks in July if that's OK.'
(.............................. REQUEST)

3 'Mr Lee had just taken off his regulation cap and gloves when his hair got caught in the machine.'
(.............................. REPORT)

4 'It tells you about your pay, hours, holidays, pension, and discipline procedures.'
(STATEMENT OF TERMS OF ....)

5 'The duties attached to this post are as follows . . .'
(.............................. DESCRIPTION)

6 'He's been away sick three times already this month.'
(.............................. RECORD)

7 'Brigitte wants two weeks in August but that's the time everyone else wants as well.'
(.............................. PLANNER)

8 'There's a vacancy in the IT department which I wouldn't mind trying for.'
(.............................. FORM)

9 'I tell her about how far I think I've achieved my objectives during the past year and she writes it all down and then we talk about next year.'
(.............................. FORM)

10 'He got it for failing to follow instructions and because he broke the health and safety rules.'
(EMPLOYEE .... NOTICE)

11 'They are usually because of retirement or resignation but occasionally we have to do one for misconduct.'
(.............................. NOTICE)

42 Socialising

Fit the two halves of each dialogue into the right places in each picture.

1 I'm sorry, I'm not feeling too good today.

2 Thanks for a wonderful evening.

3 It's not too bad today.

4 Please take a seat.

5 Where exactly do you come from?

6 How was the journey?

7 I hope you didn't have too many problems finding us.

8 How is the meal?

9 I'm in Chemicals.

10 Have you heard the news?

11 The drinks are on me.

a) So am I.

b) I'm afraid we got lost a couple of times.

c) No, you must let me pay this time.

d) Oh, I'm sorry to hear that.

e) Why, what's happened?

f) Better than yesterday.

g) The lobster is wonderful.

h) I'm glad you enjoyed it.

i) Oh, you've probably never heard f it.

j) Thank you.

k) The plane was delayed again.

43 Politics

Match the political terms and issues (1–12) with the statements (a–l).

1 Central government is too strong.

2 Local government is too strong.

3 The government has a big parliamentary majority.

4 The ruling coalition is getting weaker and weaker.

5 Homelessness is a big problem.

6 People are worried about immigration.

7 People are worried about law and order.

8 The State social security system is in debt.

9 People want a referendum on this question.

10 The civil service is too big.

11 The head of State is popular.

12 Members of Parliament – and politicians in general – are unpopular.

a) The president is liked by many people, but of course he doesn't have much real power.

b) There are too many people trying to come to this country to live.

c) The government is going to fall if the Social Democrats and the Independent Socialists don't stop arguing all the time.

d) The government can always win a vote in the Lower House and so it thinks it can do what it likes.

e) The police should be catching more criminals and the courts should be sending more of them to prison for longer.

f) They're all as bad as each other – they're just in it for themselves.

g) We have young people living rough on the streets of our cities – it's a scandal.

h) h) The government is paying out more money in pensions and welfare benefits than it's getting in.

i) We want power moved away from the big government ministries and away from the capital city.

j) There are too many government bureaucrats.

k) Our city council can do whatever it likes. The government should have more control over it.

l) We should have a direct say on this – it shouldn't be left to the politicians in Parliament to decide.

44 The economy

Match what people are saying (1–13) about the economy with what the experts say (a–m).

1 Things seem to be getting a bit better at last – better than last year at any rate.

2 At least prices aren't going up as quickly as they used to.

3 But things are still far too expensive.

4 The problem nowadays is that no one can get a job.

5 The only new factories round here belong to foreigners.

6 The government just won't put any money into business.

7 And even if you do manage to get a job, it's not in a factory.

8 It's more likely to be serving hamburgers in some fast food place.

9 And either way, the union can't do anything for you.

10 No one's got the qualifications for the jobs you see advertised in the papers.

11 I reckon we've got less in the bank than we had a couple of years ago.

12 And now they say we're going to have to start paying to go into hospital.

13 I wouldn't mind a bit more taken off my pay if I thought it would mean a bit more for schools and hospitals.

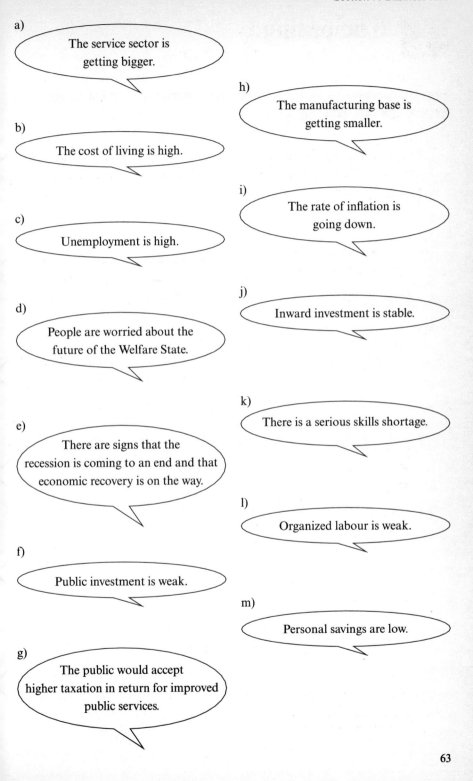

a) The service sector is getting bigger.

b) The cost of living is high.

c) Unemployment is high.

d) People are worried about the future of the Welfare State.

e) There are signs that the recession is coming to an end and that economic recovery is on the way.

f) Public investment is weak.

g) The public would accept higher taxation in return for improved public services.

h) The manufacturing base is getting smaller.

i) The rate of inflation is going down.

j) Inward investment is stable.

k) There is a serious skills shortage.

l) Organized labour is weak.

m) Personal savings are low.

45 Computing

Sidney has been away for a few years. Help Anthea explain to him about his new computer by selecting the right words or phrases from the box.

click	copy	delete	disk	file	icons
menus	mouse	personal computer		point	printer
save	select	spreadsheet		word processing	

Anthea: So where's the new PC?

Sidney: PC?

Anthea: (1) ....

Sidney: Oh, it's here. But what's this thing you're moving around with your hand?

Anthea: It's a (2) ....

Sidney: A what?

Anthea: Let's switch it on and go into Windows. Now, look at all these (3) .... on the screen.

Sidney: OK.

Anthea: If I (4) .... the cursor at one of them and then double (5) .... , I can open any of them up and take a look inside.

Sidney: And what is inside?

Anthea: Well, let's do a bit of (6) .... first – that's just a way of saying you're going to create some text.

Sidney: You mean I'm going to type something.

Anthea: That's right. You can open up a new (7) .... and then you can access any of these pull-down (8) .... like this.

Sidney: But what if I type something and make a mistake?

Anthea: You can (9) .... it like this. But it's also very
            important to (10) .... everything you produce. You can
            do that onto a (11) .... in File Manager, here.

Sidney: And if I want to move some text from one place to another?

Anthea: You (12) .... all the text you want to move and then
            move it like this. And you can also (13) .... text like this.

Sidney: And how do I get it from the screen onto paper?

Anthea: Your computer is connected to a (14) .... and so you can
            send a message to it from here.

Sidney: And what about figures? Can it add up?

Anthea: Yes, you can go into (15) .... software like this and
            create a table with columns and rows to enter figures in.

Sidney: Well, it's not bad, but can't it play any games?

46 Transport

Business people often have to talk about how they get around. Match the words in **bold** type (1–14) with the pictures (a–n).

1 I was lucky to get a seat in the **carriage**.
2 Fortunately there was plenty of room in the **restaurant car**.
3 The **high speed train** seemed to get us to the capital in no time.
4 The only holdup was when the **shuttle bus** to the aiport got stuck in heavy traffic.
5 The **jam** soon cleared.
6 The check-in was quick because I only had **hand luggage**.
7 I flew with my favourite **airline** as always.
8 On arrival, I went straight to the car hire desk to collect the **hatchback** I'd booked.
9 It's true I could have had a **saloon** this time since I had so little luggage.
10 As soon as they'd checked my **driving licence**, I was away.
11 Soon I was cruising round the **by-pass**.
12 There was a short queue at the **toll station**.
13 But it wasn't long before I was inside the **ring road** heading for the centre.
14 The hotel was right in the middle of the city's main **pedestrianised area**.

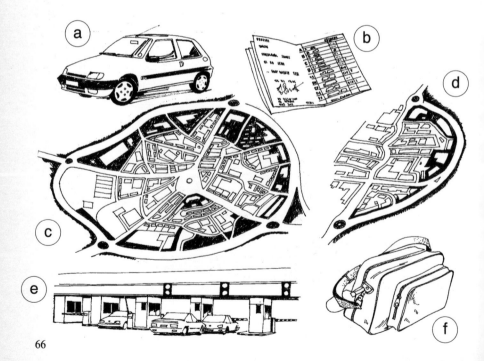

47 Figures

How do you say the following numbers? Choose the correct version in each case.

1 The year 2003:
   a) twenty hundred and three
   b) two thousand and three
   c) twenty three
   d) twenty hundred three

2 $1 = DM1.46. The exchange rate is:
   a) one point four six Deutschmarks to the dollar
   b) one forty six Deutschmarks for a dollar
   c) one dollar equalling Deutschmarks one point four six
   d) one dollar making one four six Deutschmarks

3 The period from about 1984 to about 1986:
   a) the mid-eighties
   b) the medium eighties
   c) the middling eighties
   d) the midway eighties

4 Seven correct answers in a test of ten items. The result is:
   a) seven over ten right
   b) seven out of ten right
   c) seven on ten right
   d) seven right over ten

5 The dimensions of a rectangle 3 metres in length and 2 metres in width:
   a) three for two   b) three by two   c) three across two down   d) three to two

6 The result of an opinion survey:
   a) One of ten people think that . . .
   b) One in ten people think that . . .
   c) One to ten people think that . . .
   d) One over ten people think that . . .

7 Approximately six:
   a) nearly six   b) sixish   c) sixy   d) sixer

8 At football, Germany 0, Brazil 0:
   a) Germany oh, Brazil oh
   b) Germany zero, Brazil zero too
   c) Germany nil, Brazil, nil
   d) Germany and Brazil love

9 3 cm^3:
   a) three centimetre cubes
   b) three cubic centimetres
   c) three cubed centimetres
   d) three centimetric cubes

10 3: 2 as a ratio:
   a) three over two   b) three under two   c) three to two   d) three at two

48 Business jargon

The managing director has had an attack of jargon. Help him translate his speech into plain English by substituting the words in **bold** type in each sentence (1–15) with one of the phrases (a–o).

Ladies and gentlemen

1 I want you to **take on board** a number of important points.
2 Kazoulis Communications is now a **major player** in the communications industry.
3 We work for lasting relationships with **our business partners**.
4 We employ **state-of-the-art** technology.
5 We want to produce the most **user-friendly** products on the market.
6 In our business relationships, we aim to **be proactive** every time.
7 We propose only **tailor-made** solutions.
8 We never lose sight of **the bottom line**.
9 We work hard to get **synergy** between subsidiaries.
10 We will not hesitate to **downsize** the organization for maximum efficiency.
11 We will find solutions to business problems even when **we do not have a level playing field**.
12 If anyone tries to **move the goalposts** on our commercial agreements . . .
13 . . . we will **blow the whistle**.
14 We aim to become a truly **global** operator.
15 Unfortunately I can only give you **ballpark** figures today.

a) cut the workforce of
b) business conditions are unfair
c) personalized
d) a leading company
e) change the rules (without consultation)
f) worldwide
g) the people we do business with
h) understand and accept

i) dynamic and productive relationships
j) approximate
k) anticipate needs
l) our basic objective (usually to make a profit)
m) up-to-date
n) easy-to-use
o) protest at unfair treatment

49 Sexist language

Identify the problems of the sexist language below and use one of the terms from the box to make each sentence less offensive.

appropriate clothes	artificial	chair	employees
sales representatives	Ms	spokeswoman	staff *(verb)*
staffing	their	their	women

1 Every executive knows that people will form judgements about his company on the basis of his personal behaviour.
2 We expect all our managers to wear suits and ties when on company business.
3 It is the responsibility of the chairman to ensure that meetings are conducted efficiently.
4 A spokesman for the company said that every effort was being made to implement an effective equal opportunities programme and added that she was personally convinced that it would be a success.
5 The company's manpower needs will continue to grow next year.
6 Nearly all our salesmen are against the proposed changes to the bonus system.
7 Men found guilty of sexually harassing employees of the opposite sex are liable to dismissal.
8 We have to man the assembly line on a 24-hour basis.
9 We congratulate both Mr Smith and Miss Duffy on their success in the recent sales competition.
10 If a customer complains, his complaint should be reported to the customer complaints department immediately.
11 You have to be careful what you say round here nowadays. The girls in the office downstairs might object.
12 Buy from our new range of spring clothes: made from man-made fibres but they look like the real thing!

50 Business management today

The descriptions (a–l) of each title (1–12) in the new business trends seminar series
have got mixed up. Unscramble them.

1 Business Process Re-engineering

   a) How do you turn groups of people into world-class performers? This seminar shows you how to produce focused workgroups within your business organization every time.

2 Multi-skilling

   b) The number of part-time and temporary workers is growing. What impact will this have on the culture of your organization? How can we prepare for this change?

3 Competency Development

   c) Winning teams need captains with the will to win. This seminar is led by one of our most successful national sports team captains who will tell you how to take *your* team to the top.

4 Flexible Employment

   d) Flatter organizations mean less promotion. Clear opportunities for advancement no longer exist for many managers. This seminar will help you to motivate managers who have stopped moving up the corporate ladder.

5 Downsizing the Organization

   e) Today's workers must adapt to change. They must be ready to train for new jobs not once but several times. Let this seminar help you create people who can confidently adapt to tomorrow's unpredictable world of work.

6 Leadership

   f) How do you pass on your own professional experience to a younger colleague? What are the key skills in this process? What objectives do you set?

71

What plan do you define together? Learn how to coach the managers of the future.

7 Outsourcing

g) In this seminar we look at how to reduce the size of the workforce while maintaining the loyalty and motivation of the staff who remain.

8 Mentoring

h) Tear up the company's history. Throw away the rule book and start again. By keeping a clear market focus, setting clear strategic goals and involving all the workforce fully, you can guide your company through this period of painful but necessary change.

9 Empowerment

i) We shall look at how to define the skills, attitudes and knowledge your organization needs from its people; how to establish what each employee currently has; how to measure the gap; and how to narrow it to zero.

10 Career Development

j) You can only obtain high levels of customer service from your people if they get it right first time. How do you make employees at all levels of the organization responsible for their actions? This seminar gives you the answer.

11 Benchmarking

k) You will learn how to measure practices and performances between businesses. You will increase the competitiveness of your business as a result.

12 Team Building

l) Concentrating on core business is leading more and more companies to hand over peripheral activities to specialised agencies. We shall look at the advantages and disadvantages of this approach for different kinds of non-core business.

51 Customer expectations

What do customers appreciate? What do companies aim to provide? Complete the customer-friendly adjectives below.

1 F _ S _   service

2 E _ S _   payment conditions

3 G _ N _ R _ U _   discounts

4 F _ I _ N _ L _   sales staff

5 H _ L _ F _ L   answers

6 E _ T _ A   performance

7 R _ P _ D   response

8 C _ N _ I _ T _ N _   quality

9 C _ M _ E _ I _ I _ E   prices

10 A _ S _ L _ T _   guarantees

11 L _ N _ - L _ S _ I _ G   products

12 C _ E _ R   instructions

13 F _ E _   delivery

14 C _ E _ P   insurance

15 T _ T _ L   efficiency

16 O _ E _   dialogue

17 P _ R _ O _ A _   treatment

18 U _ - T _ - D _ T _ E   information

52 Outsourcing

Kazoulis Communications wants to concentrate on its core business. Match the pictures (a–j) with the outsourced departments (1–10).

1 mail services

2 catering services

3 payroll administration

4 switchboard

5 security

6 cleaning

7 IT

8 distribution

9 storage

10 training

53 Business problems

Kazoulis Communications is in trouble. Identify the problems by unscrambling the words in capitals.

1 The number of customer C _ _ _ _ _ _ _ _ S has increased by 300% over the last six months. (SALPNITOMC)

2 Many of these relate to F _ _ _ _ Y goods. (TULYFA)

3 And also to goods D _ _ _ _ _ D in transit. (GEMADAD) ·

4 The unions say that this is because of the 30% R _ _ _ _ _ _ _ N in the workforce. (TROUNCIDE)

5 The people on the shopfloor are O _ _ _ _ _ _ _ _ _ _ _ D and can't cope. (OVDECHRETRETS)

6 The press has criticised the recent 75% P _ Y R _ _ _ S for the directors. (YAP SIRES)

7 The head of an overseas subsidiary has been caught trying to B _ _ _ E a government minister. (BERIB)

8 The Finance Director has been accused of I _ _ _ _ _ R D _ _ _ _ _ G. (INDRISE DNIGALE)

9 One of the company's main partners has recently gone B _ _ _ _ _ _ T (KRAPTUNB)

10 Kazoulis is also having cash flow problems because of S _ _ W P _ _ _ _ S. (WOLS SPYARE)

11 And then, last month, Mr Kazoulis S _ _ _ _ D the Human Resources Director. (KECDAS)

12 She has decided to sue the company for W _ _ _ _ _ _ L D _ _ _ _ _ _ _ L (GURNLOWF SMAILSIDS)

13 Since then, several senior managers have R _ _ _ _ _ _ D. (NISERDEG)

14 M _ _ _ _ E is low. (LEAROM)

15 Yesterday the computer system F _ _ _ _ D. (FLIDEA)

16 The share price has D _ _ _ _ _ D by 70%. (POPDERD)

17 Mr Kazoulis is R _ _ _ _ _ _ D to be working on a new strategic plan on an island somewhere in the Pacific. (RODURUME)

54 Business principles

Choose the best word (a–d) for each sentence to complete the following extracts from a company's mission statement.

1 We believe that business can be a powerful .... for social change.
   a) agent   b) agency   c) agenda   d) agreement

2 We affirm the need for moral .... in business decision-making.
   a) valuation   b) validity   c) values   d) valediction

3 We have a .... to shared prosperity.
   a) commission   b) commitment   c) competence   d) competition

4 Businesses have a role to .... in improving the lives of all their customers, employees and shareholders.
   a) play   b) have   c) do   d) make

5 Businesses established in foreign countries should contribute to the social .... of those countries.
   a) advances   b) advantage   c) advancement   d) adventurism

6 Businesses should .... international and domestic rules.
   a) retail   b) restrict   c) repeat   d) respect

7 Businesses should .... with each other to promote the progressive liberalization of trade.
   a) corporate   b) co-operate   c) co-ordinate   d) cope

8 Businesses should .... and, where possible, improve the environment.
   a) deflect   b) insect   c) detect   d) protect

9 Businesses should .... all their customers fairly in all aspects of their business transactions.
   a) treat   b) meet   c) seat   d) repeat

10 Businesses should .... working conditions which respect each employee's health and dignity.
   a) divide   b) confide   c) provide   d) avoid

11 Businesses have a responsibility to .... relevant information to owners and investors subject only to legal requirements and competitive constraints.
   a) open   b) close   c) disclose   d) enclose

12 Businesses should .... competitive behaviour which demonstrates mutual respect among competitors.
   a) promote   b) demote   c) motivate   d) provoke

55 Managing yourself

The concepts in the box show you how to manage yourself. Write the number of each thought bubble (1–10) next to the correct word or phrase (a–j) in the box.

---

a) balance .....

b) career .....

c) learning from mistakes .....

d) motivation .....

e) recognition .....

f) reward .....

g) risk .....

h) satisfaction .....

i) self-esteem .....

j) time management .....

---

4 I need to be able to respect myself in what I do.

5 It would be boring if we never dared into the unknown in our professional lives. There must be some adventure.

6 My job is important to me but so is my family and my own private life.

7 I want to know that there is a future direction and the chance of development in my job.

8 It's important for me to enjoy what I do.

9 I shouldn't worry if I do it wrong sometimes – as long as I try to understand why it went wrong.

1 I want people – at least the people whose opinion I value – to tell me when I've done a good job.

2 I have to prioritise my tasks at the start of each day and then work through them.

3 I expect to earn the money I think I deserve for what I do.

10 I need stimulating and interesting tasks – otherwise it's hard to get involved.

Answers

Test 1
1 g)
2 l)
3 i)
4 h)
5 k)
6 e)
7 j)
8 a)
9 c)
10 b)
11 f)
12 d)

Test 2
1 –
2 to
3 after
4 with
5 with
6 to
7 –
8 on
9 –
10 out
11 –
12 in

Test 3
Across
1 credit card
5 exchange rate
6 in the black
7 in the red
8 interest
10 withdraw
11 statement
13 pay in
Down
2 travellers cheques
3 direct debit
4 overdrawn
9 balance
12 transfer

Test 4
1 h)

2 k)
3 e)
4 g)
5 i)
6 j)
7 a)
8 b)
9 f)
10 d)
11 c)

Test 5
1 primary school
2 secondary school
3 applied
4 place, study
5 scholarship
6 subject
7 graduated
8 honours degree
9 stay on
10 higher degree
11 option
12 grant
13 thesis
14 PhD
15 job

Test 6
1 a)
2 a)
3 b)
4 a)
5 a)
6 a)
7 b)
8 a)
9 b)
10 a)
11 b)
12 b)
13 b)
14 a)
15 b)

Test 7
1 Overhead Projector
2 Video Cassette Recorder
3 Headquarters
4 Return On Investment

5 Personal Computer
6 Chief Executive Officer
7 John Fitzgerald Kennedy
   (New York Airport)
8 Gross National Product
9 Desk Top Publishing
10 Master in Business Administration
11 Annual General Meeting
12 Value Added Tax
13 Unique Selling Proposition
14 Any Other Business

Test 8
1 b) *do* a profit
2 b) *make* business
3 d) *take* a deadline
4 a) *have* progress
5 c) *meet* an appointment
6 d) *launch* progress
7 c) *complete* a cheque
8 a) *carry out* an agreement
9 a) *achieve* progress
10 b) *reach* a strategy
(Other verbs are also possible.)

Test 9
1 generates
2 sends
3 cuts
4 meets
5 bends
6 runs
7 makes
8 implements
9 reaches
10 plays
11 launches
12 signs
13 increases

Test 10
1 conveniently
2 totally
3 extensively
4 unfairly
5 satisfactorily

6 actively
7 financially
8 deeply
9 tactfully
10 highly
11 absolutely

Test 11
1 on
2 to
3 under, over
4 between
5 in
6 on
7 on
8 into
9 at, in
10 by, at
11 in
12 on

Test 12
1 open up a market / open a letter
2 stand drinks (for everyone) / stand for an elected post
3 share prices fall / trees fall down in storms
4 fill in a form / (be) fill(ed) with a sense of pride
5 cut down on cigarettes / cut costs
6 lay off workers / lay foundations
7 break bad news (to someone) / break up inefficient companies
8 sell off parts of a company / sell goods at a discount
9 kick yourself / kick off a meeting
10 take on extra staff / take too long
11 pick the best person / a market can pick up
12 bring up a problem at a meeting / bring dynamism to the job
13 carry out duties / carry news

Test 13
1 valued
2 high
3 competitive
4 right
5 future
6 large
7 critical
8 easy
9 accurate
10 guaranteed
11 mixed
12 positive
13 verbal

Test 14

Verb	Person noun	General noun	Adjective
administer	administrator	administration	administrative
distribute	distributor	distribution	distributive
advise	adviser / advisor	advice	advisory
construct	constructor	construction	constructive
pay	payer/ee	payment	payable
solve	solver*	solution	soluble
inspect	inspector	inspection	–
promote	promoter	promotion	promotional
co-ordinate	co-ordinator	co-ordination	–
supervise	supervisor	supervision	supervisory
finance	financier	finance	financial

(* e.g. problem-solver)

Test 15
1 personnel
2 address
3 appraisal
4 accommodation
5 separate
6 recommend
7 organise, organize (both spellings are acceptable)
8 stationery, stationary (both acceptable: *stationery* is writing materials such as envelopes, pens and paper; *stationary* means not moving)
9 principle, principal (both acceptable: a *principle* is a moral rule or moral standard; *principal*, as an adjective, means first in importance)
10 systematic
11 negotiation
12 commercial
13 hierarchy
14 enterprise

SECTION 3:
BUSINESS FUNCTIONS

Test 16
1 operating
2 spare capacity
3 installed
4 robots, assembly line
5 suppliers
6 component
7 just-in-time, order, consignment
8 delivery
9 conveyor belts
10 safety manager
11 quality manager
12 faulty goods

Test 17
1 g)
2 i)
3 l)
4 h)
5 j)
6 d)
7 b)
8 p)
9 m)
10 e)
11 a)
12 o)
13 k)
14 c)
15 f)
16 n)

Test 18
1 d)
2 b)
3 a)
4 b)
5 b)
6 d)
7 b)
8 a)

9 b)
10 d)
11 c)
12 c)

Test 19
1 dividend
2 bankrupt
3 margins
4 debt
5 profits
6 currency
7 charges
8 rates
9 issue
10 buyout
11 flow
12 losses

Test 20
Across
1 settlement
4 judgement
5 lease
7 liability
8 contract
11 illegal
12 breach
Down
2 legislation
3 sue
6 article
7 landlord
9 tenant
10 patent
13 costs

Test 21
1 spending
2 corporate
3 evaluation
4 performance
5 policy
6 resources
7 programmes
8 costs
9 centres
10 budget
11 outsourcing

Test 22
1 war
2 policy
3 match
4 undercutting
5 share

6 cost
7 bulk
8 margins
9 overheads
10 shakeout
11 players
12 retail
13 overcharging
14 grocery
15 down

SECTION 4:
BUSINESS EXPRESSION

Test 23
1 piloting
2 billing
3 conferences
4 fringe benefits
5 manuals
6 redundancy
7 overheads
8 bargaining
9 hunches
10 drawbacks
11 regulations
12 exhibitions

Test 24
1 b) is to take a general view; the others are about what you do when you make sure that, for example, a product or someone's work is up to the right standard.
2 c) is the opposite of promote: the others lead to job loss.
3 d) is looking at a current situation; the others are about looking at the future.
4 a) means to stop someone working; the others are about starting people working.
5 d) means to bring something back to the state it was in before; the others are about reformulating written text.
6 a) gives a list of events according to the time when they will take place; the others do not necessarily give specific times.
7 c) are about events delayed

to another time; the others are about things you must not do.
8 a) is about a planned event which will not now take place; the others are about events delayed to a later time.
9 b) is when you can't reach someone by phone because they are already using the phone; the others mean that that person is doing something else.
10 d) is used when you want to approach someone whom you don't know or interrupt someone; the others are responses to thanks.
11 a) is just before 6 o'clock; the others can be either just before or just after 6 o'clock.

Test 25
1 a) subsidy   b) subsidiary
2 a) politics   b) policy
3 a) economics   b) economic
4 a) economy   b) economies
5 a) complemental
  b) complimentary
6 a) note   b) notice
7 a) morale   b) moral
8 a) security   b) safety
9 a) take over   b) overtake

Test 26
1 cons
2 weaknesses
3 fall
4 reduce
5 loss
6 contract
7 withdraw
8 peripheral
9 fire
10 decline
11 divest
12 lay off

Test 27
1 f)
2 h)
3 i)
4 j)
5 e)

SECTION 5: BUSINESS SECTORS

Test 32

```
X V L D I S T R I B U T O R K D S P J B
S S M E F H O O L G O J M N I O B O C B
T T F D I N E T U V K I H S N C A P A M
G C U T O N G A J W Q O K A D L C Q W P
B H A E A P B U F U P X T M O R V S I
I R S R T I L P E A F Q E N P O J A M
M A C I N O B O D E L Z L L R I Q D K O
E W O R R Q U I A D I G K L Y Q Y R X V
D O T A N S B D M A T H G I H S Z X L I
I P F O J E H P O C Y A J T T F E S Y E
A U R G I K R R Q E P C B E F G U W N A
E L C V E E D E A B R D I J Z A V M V H
M I H A N T Y S C H E E C H A N N E L S
P V J P B A W S P A S H F U V T B U M L
I M K R V L Y N O X S I C H A T S H O W
R E N O W L E W W A G Y B G Z S C T W J
E R S L U M S M F C O M M E R C I A L S
T E N S L T E N O N E X U P H Q T S D X
U B R O A D C A S T F O V I T U R Z I G
Z C O R Y D R P J Z Y G A M E S H O W K
```

SECTION 6: BUSINESS COMMUNICATION

Test 36
1 i)
2 e)
3 g)
4 f)
5 a)
6 h)
7 j)
8 b)
9 c)
10 d)

Test 37
1 c)
2 e)
3 i)
4 l)
5 g)
6 b)
7 j)
8 d)
9 k)
10 a)
11 h)
12 f)

Test 38
1 o)
2 g)
3 p)
4 r)
5 b)
6 m)
7 j)
8 f)
9 n)
10 c)
11 a)
12 h)
13 i)
14 q)
15 k)
16 e)
17 d)
18 s)
19 l)

Test 39
1 up (correct)
2 back (correct)
3 through
4 down (correct)
5 on (correct)
6 off
7 through
8 up

9 up
10 back

Test 40
1 k)
2 e)
3 i)
4 d)
5 g)
6 f)
7 b)
8 j)
9 a)
10 c)
11 h)

Test 41
1 maternity
2 holiday
3 accident
4 employment
5 job
6 attendance
7 holiday
8 application
9 appraisal (or assessment)
10 warning
11 termination

Test 42
1 (9–a)
2 (6–k)
3 (7–b)
4 (1–d)
5 (10–e)
6 (11–c)
7 (3–f)
8 (5–i)
9 (2–h)
10 (4–j)
11 (8–g)

SECTION 7:
BUSINESS TALK

Test 43
1 i)
2 k)
3 d)
4 c)
5 g)
6 b)
7 e)
8 h)
9 l)
10 j)

11 a)
12 f)

Test 44
1 e)
2 i)
3 b)
4 c)
5 j)
6 f)
7 h)
8 a)
9 l)
10 k)
11 m)
12 d)
13 g)

Test 45
1 personal computer
2 mouse
3 icons
4 point
5 click
6 word processing
7 file
8 menus
9 delete
10 save
11 disk
12 select
13 copy
14 printer
15 spreadsheet

Test 46
1 m)
2 j)
3 n)
4 g)
5 i)
6 f)
7 l)
8 h)
9 a)
10 b)
11 d)
12 e)
13 c)
14 k)

Test 47
1 b)
2 a)
3 a)
4 b)

5 b)
6 b)
7 a)
8 c)
9 b)
10 c)

Test 48
1 h)
2 d)
3 g)
4 m)
5 n)
6 k)
7 c)
8 l)
9 i)
10 a)
11 b)
12 e)
13 o)
14 f)
15 j)

Test 49
1 *their* instead of *his* ('All executives know ...')
2 *appropriate clothes* instead of *suits and ties*
3 *chair* instead of *chairman*
4 *spokeswoman* instead of *spokesman*
5 *staffing* instead of *manpower*
6 *sales representatives* instead of *salesmen*
7 *employees* instead of *men*
8 *staff* instead of *man*
9 *Ms* instead of *Miss*
10 *their* instead of *his* ('If customers complain ...')
11 *women* instead of *girls*
12 *artificial* instead of *man-made*

SECTION 8:
BUSINESS MANAGEMENT

Test 50
1 h)
2 e)
3 i)
4 b)
5 g)
6 c)
7 l)
8 f)

9 j)
10 d)
11 k)
12 a)

Test 51
1 fast
2 easy
3 generous
4 friendly
5 helpful
6 extra
7 rapid
8 consistent
9 competitive
10 absolute
11 long-lasting
12 clear
13 free
14 cheap
15 total
16 open
17 personal
18 up-to-date

Test 52
1 h)
2 f)
3 a)
4 i)
5 g)
6 j)
7 b)
8 d)
9 e)
10 c)

Test 53
1 complaints
2 faulty
3 damaged
4 reduction
5 overstretched
6 pay rises
7 bribe
8 insider dealing
9 bankrupt
10 slow payers
11 sacked
12 wrongful dismissal
13 resigned
14 morale
15 failed
16 dropped
17 rumoured

Test 54
1 a)
2 c)
3 b)
4 a)
5 c)
6 d)
7 b)
8 d)
9 a)
10 c)
11 c)
12 a)

Test 55
1 e)
2 j)
3 f)
4 i)
5 g)
6 a)
7 b)
8 h)
9 c)
10 d)

Word List

The numbers after the entries are the tests in which they appear.

A

about, 24
absolute guarantee, 51
absolutely certain, 10
accident, 30
accident report, 41
accommodation, 15
accumulation, 33
accurate figures, 13
achieve a breakthrough, 8
achieve a target, 8
achieve little, 8
actively seeking, 10
address, 15
administration, 14
advancement, 54
advise, 14
agent, 54
airline, 46
all over the world, 6
analyse, 24, 33
Annual General Meeting, 7
anticipate, 24
any other business, 7
application form, 41
apply, 5
appraisal, 15, 18
appraisal form, 41
appropriate clothes, 49
appropriate dress, 37
approximately, 47
around, 24
article, 20
artificial fibre, 49
ask for clarification, 38
assembly line, 16
assure, 30
at the latest, 11
at this stage, 11
attendance record, 41
audience, 35
auditor, 1
automotive, 28

B

balance, 3, 55
ballpark figure, 48
ban, 24

bank crisis, 31
bank manager, 1
bankrupt, 19, 53
bargaining, 23
be involved in, 2
benchmarking, 50
bend rules, 9
beneficiary, 30
billing, 23
biotechnology, 34
blend, 33
blockbuster, 34
blow the whistle, 48
body language, 37
bonus, 18
bottom line, 48
brand, 17
breach, 20
break, 12
break up, 12
bribe, 53
bring, 12
bring up, 12
broadcast, 32
brochure, 17
broker, 30
budget, 21
bulk, 22
business process re-engineering, 50
busy, 24
buyout, 19
by-pass, 46
by the end of the month, 11

C

cable, 32
call back, 39
campaign, 17
cancel, 24
career, 55
career development, 50
carriage, 46
carry, 12
carry out, 2, 12, 33
carry out a market survey, 8
carry out a plan, 8
carry out research, 8
cash flow, 19

catering, 28
catering services, 52
Central Europe, 6
central government, 43
centre, 21
chair, 49
channel, 32
charges, 19
chat show, 32
cheap insurance, 51
check, 24, 38
Chief Executive Officer, 7
civil engineer, 1
civil servant, 1
civil service, 43
claim, 30
cleaning, 52
clear instruction, 51
click, 45
clinical trial, 34
close, 36
close a meeting, 38
close to retirement, 11
coalition, 43
come down in price, 22
commercial, 15, 32
commission, 4
commitment, 54
commodities, 31
competency development, 50
competitive price, 13, 51
complaint, 53
complementary, 25
complete a form, 8
complete a project, 8
complete a task, 8
complimentary, 25
component, 16
conference, 23, 35
conglomerate, 34
consignment, 16
consistent quality, 51
construction, 28
constructor, 14
consumer electronics, 28
contract, 20, 26
contribution, 30
control, 24